The Gr Chagford Book

Chips Barber

Illustrations: Jane Reynolds

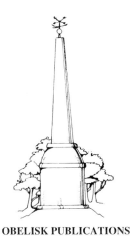

OBELISK PUBLICATIONS

ALSO BY THE AUTHOR

Diary of a Dartmoor Walker / Diary of a Devonshire Walker
The Great Little Dartmoor Book / The Great Little Exeter Book
The Great Little Plymouth Book / The Great Little Totnes Book
The Lost City of Exeter
Beautiful Dartmoor / Beautiful Exeter
Torbay in Colour / Plymouth in Colour
Made in Devon *(with David FitzGerald)*
Dark and Dastardly Dartmoor *(with Sally Barber)*
Weird and Wonderful Dartmoor *(with Sally Barber)*
Ghastly and Ghostly Devon *(with Sally Barber)*
The Ghosts of Exeter *(with Sally Barber)*
Ten Family Walks on Dartmoor *(with Sally Barber)*
Ten Family Walks in East Devon *(with Sally Barber)*
Burgh Island and Bigbury Bay *(with Judy Chard)*
Tales of the Teign *(with Judy Chard)*
Dawlish and Dawlish Warren
Torquay / Paignton / Brixham
The South Hams
Around & About Salcombe
Around & About Seaton and Beer
Around & About Sidmouth
Around & About Teignmouth and Shaldon
Topsham Past and Present
From The Dart to The Start
Dartmouth and Kingswear
Cranmere Pool – The First Dartmoor Letterbox
The Teign Valley of Yesteryear

For further details of these or any of our titles, please send an SAE to Obelisk Publications at the address below, or telephone Exeter 468556.

Acknowledgements
Thanks to the members of the Webber family,
Mrs Cosford, Mr and Mrs Rowe, and Mr Smith of Whipton PO

*First published in 1994. Reprinted 1997
by Obelisk Publications, 2 Church Hill, Pinhoe, Exeter, Devon
Designed by Chips and Sally Barber
Typeset by Sally Barber
Printed in Great Britain by
The Devonshire Press Limited, Torquay, Devon*

The Great Little Chagford Book

The Great Little Chagford Book

Chagford is a special place in many respects. For a village with a population of about 1,500 it has certainly made an impact on the life and history of the county of Devon. Dwarfed by one of Devon's biggest hills, this is a place full of character, an inland resort for the more discerning type of visitor. Despite its lack of size and relative remoteness, it has many hotels and an assortment of individual shops.

Amongst these select shops are Webbers and Bowdens, two businesses that compete with a friendly rivalry, having been on the scene for several generations. In fact it is true that this book only exists because of the Webbers and their staff's enthusiasm to see Chagford represented in print, so as these have played their parts in the social and economic history of this moorland town, it's with no apologies that we begin with them.

I consulted guide books going back to 1925 and Webbers are prominent in each and every one, their promise of supplying almost every domestic need imaginable ensuring their trading success through thick and thin.

When 'Dr Who' visited Chagford and visited Webbers he must have thought that he had found that his 'Tardis' was not the only one as this shop with a relatively small frontage is deceptive, being extremely spacious internally.

Webbers have been trading at Chagford since 1898. Gideon Webber, who was a Chagford man, but in temporary exile in London, heard that Walter Thorn had put his saddler's business up for sale. Realising its potential, he bought it to set up 'Webber & Sons'. It dawned on him that he could extend his saddlery business by adding hardware items, cycles and even travel goods. After all there were encouraging signs that tourism was going to be something of a moneyspinner with Chagford seeing a steady growth in guest houses and hotels at that time. Although more will be said later of Chagford's transport, Webbers were appointed as an agent for the London & South Western Railway. For those whose horizons were more modest, and who needed to cycle to their destinations, their path also lead to Webbers as they were also agents for Raleigh.

As more people got motor cars a need for a supply of petrol arose. As petrol stations were still to be a thing of the future, those elite few who had cars called at Webbers with their petrol cans to have them filled at the shop!

In the early pioneering days of radio and records Webbers also sold wireless sets that were made in the shop and phonographs that would be regarded as museum pieces today.

At the back of this enormous shop is a store that could no doubt tell a few stories of its own. Gideon Webber started converting stables into a hall for Chagfordians to have an extra meeting place. Unfortunately he was killed in an accident in 1916 and it was never completed in the way that he intended. However, the Central Hall, as it became known, was a venue for a wide range of activities from the joys of Scouts, Girl Guides, magic lantern shows, and dances to the miseries of accommodating the dreaded dentist.

Another shop in the Square

Frederick Webber took over the reins of the business and developed it into a thriving one. During the Second World War he incorporated the adjacent premises of Collins the butcher and Perrott the fishing tackle specialist. The expansion allowed further growth and the range of items is considerable. The firm of Webbers is a family one in every sense, one that is based on personal good service that is set to continue for many more years.

Bowdens have also been around for many years and is another of surprising size internally. In the mid 1980s a museum was formed within a part of the shop. It takes the form of a shop within a shop, but the reconstructed shop frontage of the original Bowden's is one to only gaze through in order to see the various local treasures and artifacts behind the window. It has been lovingly assembled and is intended to also be a memorial to Agnes Clara Bowden (Aunt Aggie), Thomas Reginald Bowden (Uncle Tom), Winifred Grace Mary Aggett Smith (Winnie) and Paul Wimborne Smith (Jack).

Within is a variety of items from a bygone age, household wares of all types that will rekindle memories for older generations whilst probably amusing those not quite so far along life's tempestuous path. And there are also items of specific interest like a board showing Chagford's Market tolls. In addition to several old photos of Chagford, there

is a portrait of Dick Perrott, a son of the famous James Perrott, who was responsible, albeit unwittingly, of starting the craze for Dartmoor letterboxing. Outside the display is a visitors' book and a letterbox stamp for those who want an easier introduction to this addictive Dartmoor hobby.

Originally James Bowden & Son was established as the Vulcan Ironworks, in 1862. This was a time when there was plenty of work in the Chagford area for the manufacture of agricultural machinery and equipment. Repairs were also carried out but the needs of customers led to the establishing of an ironmonger's shop. Chagfordians are fortunate to have such amazing shops for so small a population!

When R. T. Gough ran a newsagent's shop in The Square their advert, in an old Chagford guide book, included a bit of the Devonshire vernacular stating, "Give us yer order. If us ab'm got 'un us'll zoon get 'un."

Chagford Post Office is another institution with a long family connection. The name of Thorn has been synonymous with it for several generations. Originally it was housed in a cottage in Lower Street. It has had various locations since but post office business has been transacted in the present premises since the turn from the nineteenth to the twentieth century at the present location. Although the post office has ticked over throughout the years, there have been occasional scares. In 1911 it was struck by a flash of lightning during one of those terrific thunderstorms that sometimes reverberate around the Dartmoor hills.

In the past when telegraphs were the most swift form of communication, messages had to be taken down here and then communicated to the outlying farms and homesteads of the district. During the First World War, the postmistress, Mrs Sleep, had the unenviable task of delivering the dreaded pink envelopes that bore tragic news for their recipients. One of those reluctant journeys took her all the way out to Teignhead Farm, which was then an occupied farm, to pass on bad news to the Hutchings. Such harrowing errands are not part and parcel of the brief today as the Thorn connection continues with Douglas, who is a well-known figure in Chagford's community.

Chagford is often fondly referred to as "Chaggyford" by many locals. The first part of the name refers to rough vegetation, in the form of gorse, and the latter part means a crossing place. Therefore one can make the assumption that this place developed on rough land that gently rolled down to a suitable crossing place over the River Teign. Probably the moorland nature of Meldon Hill once extended down to the Teign.

The village lies about a mile off the main road that runs up a large fault valley from Bovey Tracey and on in the direction of Okehampton. Notice how we don't say Moretonhampstead, for it's Chagford's rival! Actually of a similar size, history relates several tales of the 'friendly' rivalry with it from debates about which has the better sportsmen through to the quality of shops and pubs. During the Second World War it is believed that one Moretonhampstead wag wrote on his town's gasometer, in enormous letters, "Chagford 5 miles", with an arrow to show German planes the way there!

Chagford has proved that it is no ordinary place and has been singled out for media

6

coverage on a number of occasions and for a variety of purposes. In November 1980 the popular radio programme "Down Your Way" paid a visit. The late Brian Johnston ("the bowler's Holding, the batsman's Willey") that immensely amusing and amused cricket commentator, who was dismissed for 81 to enter that great pavilion in the sky (Lord's?) in early 1994, was the master of ceremonies for a broadcast that reflected the flavour and feel of the place.

The local personalities entrusted with painting this portrait of the spoken word to the nation included local historian Jane Hayter-Hames; Johnny Arden, a well-known horse driving teacher; Tony Bennett, who left not only his heart but his bird refuge in Chagford; and Ralph Faulkner who was then head of the Primary School. Among the gems of local interest he imparted was the fact that the school band's instruments were the very ones used by the Devonshire Regiment as they made their triumphant march into Berlin at the end of the war, the regiment having borrowed them from Chagford's band in the first instance. The last guest was Mr Dick Collins who rounded the show up by describing the delights of living in such a special place as Chagford.

Chagford is twinned with the town of Bretteville-sur-Laize in Calvados, Normandy. The twinning charter was signed in May 1975 and a banquet was held at the former Moor Park Hotel to set the wheels (or 'les roues') in motion. There have been many cultural and sporting exchanges and a wander around the streets of this small French town, that bears similarities to its Dartmoor counterpart, will undoubtedly lead you to "Rue de Chagford" – home from home! And a comparable stroll around Chagford will locate Bretteville Close.

However, when people first enter Chagford, apart from noticing its French twin, they see it enjoys a status also enjoyed by three other Dartmoor towns, that of being an ancient stannary town, one of four that received Dartmoor's tin. The word derives from the Latin word 'stannum', which means tin. Dartmoor was divided into four quarters and Chagford, a parish with more than its fair share of this once more relatively important mineral, became the tin town on the north eastern margin of the moor in 1328.

Tin was initially taken from the surface but the best tin ores lay a long way below ground. Chagford was well placed to receive the tin from a number of mines in the district.

Great Weeke lies just to the east of Chagford. Today it is a quiet backwater where the pace of life is more serene than it was in the years between 1887–1892 when 'Consuls' was a scene of hectic industrial activity. In that brief period the mine produced more than fifty tons of tin. At times of heavy prolonged spells of rain, production was halted as the workings became flooded.

Vitifer Mine, near the Warren House Inn, also had its problems, probably more so as this was located on higher ground where the extremes of weather were greater. On one occasion the miners could not go to work because of snow so amused themselves in Chagford. However when the weather relented they went back to Vitifer to discover the rise in temperatures had lead to a rapid thaw and the mine was flooded to a great depth. As it is more than likely that several of them would have been drowned, they gave their thanks. It is believed that one token of their gratitude at being spared, is the 'pig' on the church roof.

Whilst the tinners toiled below in the bowels of the moor, sheep grazed unconcernedly on the hillsides far above. These were the mainstay of another Chagford industry, the manufacture of wool. A large woollen mill was established here in 1800 by Mr Berry, a large property owner, of Ashburton. At its peak more than a thousand people were employed in this trade, which was based at a number of sites. The higher factory had two large buildings and the lower factory was where the tuckers, weavers and combers went to work processing the wool.

Chagford cornered the market in this part of Devon and sheep from a vast area provided fleeces for what was, for many years, a lucrative trade. Serge and blankets were manufactured and then carried away to Ashburton or Buckfastleigh, in a good week as many as seven hundred being produced. In *Diary of a Devonshire Walker* there is a vivid description of my friends' and my attempt to retrace the 'jobbers' or wool carriers' steps. Although it makes interesting reading, it also rekindles memories of the days when I thought nothing of walking thirty miles in a day – and I don't think much of it now either!

More than a hundred men were employed at Chagford, these being called to work by a bell that was tolled definitely for them! Years later this bell was moved to a chapel at Postbridge to call people, this time the vicar's flock, to worship.

The wool trade endured fluctuating fortunes, market forces dictating productivity and occasional closures. After many ups and downs it finally ceased production in 1880.

However sheep kept coming to Chagford for its regular markets. Originally they were held in The Square but a purpose-built market nearby reduced the congestion in the shopping area.

Chagford's livestock market, near The Square, was once a scene of much activity and at its peak it was common for up to two thousand animals to arrive there. Such was the competition to get into the early part of the action that some farmers would bring their animals in at 4 a.m., using lanterns to get the best pens. In an average year there were seven market days, the majority on the Tuesday before the first Thursday of the month. Alas this market closed on 28 November 1991, to allow the site to be redeveloped. The market has been relocated at Crannafords on the outskirts of Chagford and continues with a similar frequency.

About 1890 one of the two sites involved in the woollen industry was taken over by Mr Reed who set up a saw milling operation. In addition he crushed oats, the power being harnessed from running water to make an early hydroelectric plant. The fourteen-foot breast undershot waterwheel, driven by the waters of the Teign that had been diverted into a quarter mile long leat, worked a lighting plant operating at 2,000 volts to light the town from 1st September 1891. This was the same year that Devon had been, from early March through to May, under siege from the Great Blizzard. George Reed was a resourceful man and his electricity was carried up the hill to the town by single core, lead-covered and paper-insulated cable that ran in wooden ducts. It was used to light houses and the streets. There were some folk who were so amazed to see this oasis of light illuminating the night skies that they climbed distant hills to gaze in awe at Chagford. As there was no way the electricity could be metered, a fixed charge of £1 per quarter per lamp was made. In order to step the supply down, earthenware transformers were placed in strategic locations around the town. There was even one planted in a convenient hole in the church wall!

This is just one of several examples to show that Chagford has often been at the forefront of technology 'light years' ahead of its time!

Not long after, in January 1893, a scheme at Yeo Farm to generate power for an amazing variety of uses was a real achievement. A leat from the River Teign turned a thirteen-foot overshot waterwheel that, in turn, drove a dynamo. By day this versatile system worked a flour mill, a bone mill, circular saws, laundry machines and even boot cleaning brushes! For years the farm acted as a corn mill with all the equipment to make it function, all cleverly conceived and constructed.

But what of the family behind such a futuristic scheme? The Perrymans were well known in the district, the family having been there for several generations. John Perryman pioneered the technological innovations, his son William modified them and Wallace Perryman carried on the good work. At one time they employed about seventy people, at Yeo, which made the activities a harmonious mix of agricultural and industrial pursuits.

The fields were littered in granite rocks – these were removed to improve the land and a mason carved them for granite setts to be used along the streets of Exeter as paving stones. The corporation, at Exeter, liked the materials produced at Yeo Farm, the only inconvenience being the lack of a railway to convey them to Devon's county town.

The various enterprises at Yeo have ultimately led several television presenters to visit, right up until the time the last Perryman left the farm. Celebrities like Clive Gunnell, Hugh Scully and Julian Pettifer all felt there was sufficient interest here to present to a wider audience.

The vibes of this may have influenced another young man who worked at Highfield in Chagford. Frank Whittle is the answer to the frequently heard pub quiz question as to whom is responsible for the invention of the jet engine. He spent some years in this moorland town and is credited with his achievement in 1930 at the age of just 23!

Another use of granite occurred in 1904 when a six-ton block was removed and taken all the way to Pirbright in Surrey. This was at the request of Lady Stanley who wanted to erect a fitting monument to her husband, Sir Henry Morton Stanley, the celebrated African explorer. He, it was, who was sent to find Dr Livingstone, we presume, at the request of James Gordon Bennett. He successfully completed his task at Ujiji and later followed the Congo (Zaire) to the sea.

The great slab (and five smaller stones) at his grave are all from the neighbourhood of

Chagford. The great stone was twelve feet long and varied in width between two and four feet. For years it had formed part of a fence lying in a recumbent position at Frenchbeer Farm, about a mile from Fernworthy Reservoir. Three of its sides had been exposed to the elements and were well weathered and was thus was regarded as ideal. Robert Stark, the owner and George Mortimer, the tenant, were happy to part with the stone provided that a small brass plate was affixed to the spot from where it had been removed simply to say where and why it had gone. However, there was still the problem of conveying this monstrous rock to its destination. Crowds lined the streets of Chagford to watch the traction engine haul its mighty megalith through the town's narrow streets and on to the railway terminus at Moretonhampstead. From there the stone was taken to its final resting place.

Lady Stanley went to great lengths to get a suitable monument because her husband's African name – 'Bula Matari' means 'the Rock Breaker'. Now he lies at peace, his rock breaking all done and immortalised in the rock of all ages – Dartmoor granite!

Victorian and Edwardian Chagford saw a growth in visitors, almost unparalleled in other inland Devon towns. This description conveys what the place was like at that time.

"The streets of Chagford are very irregular, and are by no means imposing in appearance. There are no grand shop fronts and the thatched houses, which stand at all angles, are

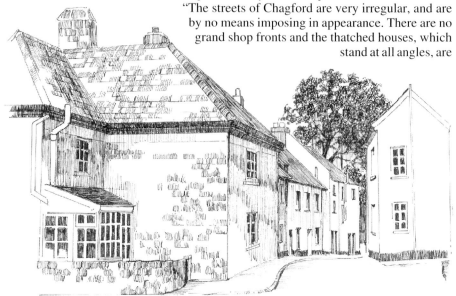

not always picturesque in effect; but whatever their structural defects, the houses present a clean and comely appearance. In no place is whitewash of a more virgin appearance; nowhere do clear muslin blinds adorn so many cottage windows; hotel managers and lodging house keepers seem to vie with each other in all that appertains to living in cleanliness and comfort; and the remainder of the population are compelled to follow suit by the force of good example."

Those discerning visitors who chose Chagford for its hunting, fishing, shooting and walking would have certainly encountered a legend in the shape of local man James Perrott. His span of life almost coincided with Queen Victoria, his life beginning and ending a few years before hers. Coincidentally he passed away on the occasion of her 76th birthday! Whilst the Industrial Revolution changed the face of much of the English landscape, Perrott trundled quietly on in a blissful pursuit of good fishing and moorland walking.

Known affectionately as 'Old Perrott' he was the local expert and there was hardly a book published about the Moor without his thoughts and advice being sought first. He took several famous people walking, amongst them the literary figures of R. D. Blackmore and Charles Kingsley. The latter was a great friend and Perrott found Kingsley's writings a comfort right up to his death in 1895. Blackmore

Perrott in The Square

introduced Perrott into some of his books so impressionable was the man. That greatest of all Dartmoor writers, William Crossing, wrote the following of him: "His knowledge of the moor rendered his conversation exceedingly interesting … The archaeologist, the searcher after the picturesque, and the angler have each been indebted to him; there was not a tor or hill in the northern part of the moor to which he could not conduct them, nor a stream in the neighbourhood in which he knew not the pools and the stickles most likely to afford sport. A deft fishermen himself, and entering keenly into the pleasures of the gentle art, he was always desirous that those who accompanied him should realise the delight of returning with a well-filled creel … We have heard him spoken of three thousand miles from Dartmoor, and the memories his name recalled, it was evident to us, were among the most cherished." High praise indeed from a man eminently qualified to know what and who he was talking about.

But all Dartmoor lovers and in particular, letterboxers, should appreciate what Perrott unwittingly started for it was this man of the moor who appreciated that great tract of wilderness country on the highest tableland of Dartmoor for what it really was, an area of remoteness and rare loveliness. It was here at a point known as Cranmere Pool, in the almost featureless fen country of the high moor, that Perrott set up, in 1854, a bottle at a cairn. The idea was pure genius. Those precious few people finding their way to the middle of nowhere would find a calling card in the bottle of the previous visitor and would remove it with the possibility of paying them a visit or simply to get in touch. Then that person would leave their own card and wait in anticipation of a call themselves, the numbers of people visiting the pool, in a year in the 1850s being but a handful. Cranmere

Pool has a place in the annals of local history as a shrine that all self-respecting walkers have to visit as part of their Dartmoor education. Indeed the bottle evolved into a 'Letterbox' eventually attaining a status such that it is recorded on Ordnance Survey maps. If you want to know more of this legendary pool, and the start of the 'letterboxing' craze, then please consult my book "Cranmere Pool – The First Dartmoor Letterbox".

The late Eric Hemery also set himself up as a Dartmoor guide operating out of Chagford in 1951. In those days there were not nearly as many guides as there are today when they seem to be almost as numerous as those who require the guiding! It is unlikely that many would have Hemery's encyclopaedic knowledge of the moor, an ability that is reflected in his mammoth tome "High Dartmoor." His advert in an old Chagford guide book ran to a whole page and took the shape of several questions. Those realising that they didn't know the answers, but would like to, could apply in person or by post to an address in Lower Street.

A sign of how things have changed since that entry more than forty years ago is one

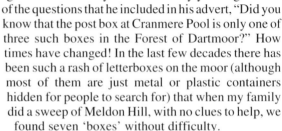

of the questions that he included in his advert, "Did you know that the post box at Cranmere Pool is only one of three such boxes in the Forest of Dartmoor?" How times have changed! In the last few decades there has been such a rash of letterboxes on the moor (although most of them are just metal or plastic containers hidden for people to search for) that when my family did a sweep of Meldon Hill, with no clues to help, we found seven 'boxes' without difficulty.

Whilst mentioning the names of acclaimed Dartmoor writers and walkers, it would be wrong not to mention the highly likable F. H. (Harry) Starkey who died in April 1989. He was a familiar face in Chagford having given a series of lectures there about Dartmoor, which inspired many to begin exploring the moor. There was a tribute to him in the second edition of the Chagford Times, which recorded his ties with the moorland town.

His retirement could not have been a bigger contrast to his working life. Harry had risen to Chief Superintendent in the Metropolitan Police but his holidays were always spent on his beloved Dartmoor. As soon as retirement was reached the lure of the moors beckoned and a bungalow at Haytor Vale provided the perfect base to continue an exploration of the moor, which spanned many years and one that he shared with many people through his talks, walks and books.

One of the lanes that Perrott and Hemery would probably have taken their charges along, on some occasions, was Tincombe Lane (originally called Featherbed Lane on account of its apparent dampness underfoot) up to the Moor. The celebrated Rev Sabine Baring-Gould included this poem about it in his "Book of Dartmoor."

Tincombe Lane is all uphill   'Tis smooth to foot, 'tis full of rut
Or downhill, as you take it;   'Tis wide and then 'tis narrow.
You tumble up and crack your crown,   Tincombe Lane is just like life
Or tumble down and break it.   From where you leave your mother;
Tincombe Lane is crooked and straight   'Tis sometimes this, 'tis sometimes that,
Here pothook, there as arrow;   'Tis one thing or another.

A favourite walk of many who stay or live in Chagford is the one beside the Teign down to Fingle Bridge. There are reasons why this particular stroll is so popular. It is the one walk in the district that doesn't demand great reserves of energy as it is, generally, a flattish route, Fingle Bridge being less high above sea level makes it a downhill walk! It is also a beautiful walk, whatever the season, and one that will revitalise the spirits provided the weather is amenable. However an old magazine article, titled "Holiday centres of the West–No. 4" and written in 1904, about this walk, once came up with these pearls of wisdom: "… leaving Chagford

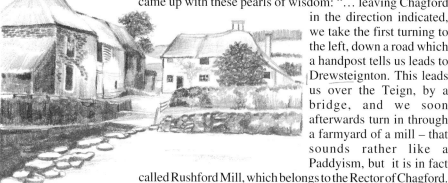

in the direction indicated, we take the first turning to the left, down a road which a handpost tells us leads to Drewsteignton. This leads us over the Teign, by a bridge, and we soon afterwards turn in through a farmyard of a mill – that sounds rather like a Paddyism, but it is in fact called Rushford Mill, which belongs to the Rector of Chagford. Getting over a dilapidated stile we follow a path by the river; but, unfortunately for ladies, we soon come to a wood, through which no harm would be done were a decent footpath made for the accommodation of visitors; but it is not done". It's a good job this wasn't written today as it would definitely be branded as both sexist and racist!

High on the hill, but hidden in woods, is an old building from the days when follies on hill tops were commonplace. Rushford Tower was built in the nineteenth century for the benefit of the wives and children who wanted to watch the local shoot. In 1883 the nearby woods were once the unlikely location for a bowling green.

Another man to appreciate the beauty of Dartmoor was William Morrish. Apart from roaming the uplands in the nineteenth century, this Chagfordian also loved painting them and today his Dartmoor landscapes are sought-after items. He had his own gallery in the Square.

As we have already seen, it would be completely wrong to say that Chagford was ever behind the times, but during the early part of the twentieth century there were definite signs that it, at least, bore a certain age-old rustic charm rather than a sophisticated swagger. Take the case of the visitor who suddenly felt uncomfortable when he realised that he was unshaven (this in an age long before 'designer stubble' was fashionable). In earnest he sought out the one and only barber and had this to say about the experience: "A mort of years ago I found myself unshaven in Chagford, the famous moorland hamlet in Devon. Inquiry for a hairdresser led me to the crowded market, where I duly found the local practitioner. I still recall that shave. The chair was an ordinary wooden kitchen one. The brush was a paintbrush, and the soap jar had a Hartley's marmalade label. But the barber was all right. When I hinted that he was, in his zeal, shaving me rather close, he apologised. Among his patrons, he said, were the local Yeomanry, who liked 'a smert zhave!'"

One of the delights of living in a community such as Chagford, in the past, was that everyone knew everybody else. People lived and worked here and it has been said that if they had built a wall around the place, not many folk would have noticed, they had so little need to leave. This sociable atmosphere rubbed off in various ways with most people's Christian names being dropped in favour of quaint nicknames. These were bestowed for a miscellany of reasons, some quite logical others on a whim. Many were fine names of people who did not stand on ceremony. Say these names out loud, preferably when there's nobody around, and see what a natural ring they have. Even though most of them are long gone it is easy to formulate a mental picture of what these real characters were like just from their nicknames: Diney Aggett, Rishy Aplin, Bangy Bennett, Fiddler Bennett, Splitfig Bolt, Fibber Cann, Polar Cousins, Pudgy Cousins, Lion Endicott, Oddle Endicott, Tackles Leaman, Toddler Leaman, Lotsol Lyddon, Snaffy Lyddon, Bucky Row, Binger Underhill, Force of Course Webber … and so on!

Up to about 1925 the streets were kept clean by Bob Cann, a task that he did cheerfully for many years. Long before the age of wheely bins Bob swept up the dirt and rubbish and deposited it into a small cart pulled by a very friendly donkey. Children on their way to school would go out of their way to find Bob and the donkey. The latter was then the recipient of a great amount of attention. The sight of this inseparable duo was the subject of a postcard – it's hard to imagine today that the corporation cart would be chosen as a vehicle on which to base a greetings card!

Another member of the family, Fibber Cann, also had the unenviable task of cleaning out the coal lorry to transform it into a conveyance with a standard of cleanliness and comfort suitable enough to carry the Chagford boys off to boarding school at Totnes in the years around 1930. Having swept the dust out he had to lay a carpet on the floor of the lorry, such adaptability being the hallmark of a less sophisticated Chagford of old.

The influx of visitors necessitated accommodation of various types and their arrival in substantial numbers gave the town a commercial boost, many local people finding work. It is worth considering some of the pubs and hotels of Chagford as many of them

14

played, and continue to play, their part, some of them not just tourist haunts but home to unpaying ghostly guests…

Chagford has two celebrated ghosts both whom share many similarities. Both lived and subsequently died in the 1640s, both were shot dead within a hundred yards of each other even though their stories are unrelated. Both too have bars named after them at the Three Crowns in High Street, a short way from The Square, one having died there. Both have made ghostly appearances there, in the 1970s, some three centuries after their early departures from this mortal coil!

Mary Whiddon was a young girl who had looked forward with great anticipation to her wedding day at Chagford's parish church on 11 October 1641. Some accounts say that her fate was decided at the altar, whilst some say that it was on emerging from the church that her short life was brought to a swift and abrupt halt. A jealous former lover could not bear to see her happy with someone else and shot her dead. Her tomb, inside the church, carries this epitaph:

Reader would'st thou know who here is laid,   A Mary for the better part
Behold a matron yet a maid   But drie thine eies, why wilt thous weep
A modeste looke, a pious heart   Such doubtless doe not die but sleepe.

However that is not quite the end of the story for the poor girl is not completely at rest and makes occasional spiritual sortees. She was sighted at Whiddon House in the early hours of the wedding day of Nigel Code, the son of the owners of the house. One of the guests had been put up in a room that had occasionally been used by the would-be bride. Harry Hayward could hardly believe his eyes as an attractive red-cheeked young lady, about 20–25 years old, stood in the doorway in the wee small hours of the morning. When he looked at her she simply smiled and faded away! The rest of the day went well and the bride acknowledged the ghostly greeting by having her bridal bouquet placed on Mary Whiddon's memorial stone.

The Goliards Amateur Theatre Company have dramatised Mary Whiddon's sad story for a short series of four performances at Shilstone Manor farm. The August 1991 production was staged in the open air in the farm's courtyard and a total of about a thousand people went to see it and were duly impressed.

The Three Crowns was originally named the Black Swan. This was the emblem of the Whiddon family granted to Sir John Whiddon, in the sixteenth century as his crest for the way he conducted himself as a judge of the Queen's Bench. There used to be a large coopering works at the back. Here hogsheads were made to contain beer or cider and quart firkins for farm workers to take to work in the fields. A hard working person could consume large amounts of potent cider without being too influenced as they sweated it out of their system by toiling long and hard – or so it is said!

The pub has other romantic attachments for it is believed that it featured in Alfred Noyse's poem "The Highwayman". Rich pickings were up for grabs on the road over the moor, or so it was reckoned. The Highwayman had a soft spot for Bess the Landlord's daughter and rode to the inn in search of her. It is believed that a spot on the B3212, known as the Watching Place, was a place of execution and that a highwayman was left to dangle in chains after he had been executed … If you walk past there you may share with many others the feeling that a pair of eyes are watching you even if there is nobody around! Bess hasn't been seen there yet. More stories like this can be found in *Dark and Dastardly Dartmoor*.

All the excitement and passion of highwaymen and tales of unrequited love was from an age when Chagford was a remote backwater far from madding crowds. The English

Civil War, which really had little place in Chagford, was one that lasted from 1642-1646. Yet it touched this rural community in a number of ways. The real losers were the ordinary folk who picked up the tab for feeding and drinking whichever troops occupied their town. Many towns in Devon changed hands

quite often and the people were resigned to the imposition that this often brought – not even tax deductible! Despite the apparent unfairness of all this, it leads us to our second Chagford ghost ...

A group of rowdy Roundheads had ensconced themselves at Chagford and the Royalists, led by Sir John Berkeley, decided to give them a hostile hello. Among the Royalist ranks was one Sidney Godolphin, an artist and a poet, described as a man of incomparable parts. In the skirmish that ensued poor Sidney was shot and died in the porch of the Three Crowns. The history books tell us that it was just above the knee where his wound was inflicted, just how far above is a delicate matter of debate for the young man, so highly regarded, died from the blast. Evidently everybody thought that his loss was a high price to pay for the taking of the town. For some reason even though Godolphin, MP for Helston in Cornwall, had relations at Chagford, he was buried at Okehampton. The three other men killed in this affray were buried at Chagford.

However Godolphin has crossed those miles of misty moorland to return to the place of his premature demise ...

Jock Hardie was stunned into silence in June 1980 when he came face to face with Sidney Godolphin, complete with all his 'incomparable parts.' In ten years as a chef there he had heard of Sidney's sorry saga many times but when he turned and clearly saw him at the door to the dining room he was taken aback. As large as life ghostly Godolphin appeared complete with a large plumed hat and full cavalier dress.

The Three Crowns achieved regional glory, in 1988, when it triumphed in an inter-pub regional television competition. The ten team members displayed their various talents at playing darts, arm wrestling, general knowledge, skittles and entertainment. The coveted title and respective cup was won in a field of 160 entries across the south west peninsular.

Had there been a round on literature they might have called on Charles Kingsley, as a guest player (had he not been dead for 113 years!) as this hotel was patronised by the famed writer. He described it as 'A Beautiful Old Mullioned and Gabled Perpendicular Inn.' Apart from the apparent ability to speak in capital letters, this quote of such a literary giant was used in the past for adverts, the notion being that a bit of name dropping was no bad thing.

Another boost to the trade of this inn many decades ago was its hostess, a lady of even more incomparable parts than Sidney Godolphin! Her capabilities were legendary and William Crossing afforded this testament to her: "This was the bright and cheery Mrs Brook, famed for her punch [presumably of the liquid variety!] her beefsteaks, and her beauty. Many a traveller in search of those attractions, with which nature has endowed this eastern borderland of Dartmoor, has had cause to congratulate himself upon having alighted upon such a house of entertainment, and such a hostess."

The Globe, a sixteenth-century coaching inn, is close by. Unlike many other places of refreshment, this was built for the purpose and was originally called the Gregory's Arms. The Azalea Room is believed to be haunted by the ghost of a former chambermaid who was deliberately drowned for being a witch.

The irony here is that witches cannot be drowned so her spiritual stirrings are probably caused by her innocent and needless death. Originally stage coaches and then buses, set off from Chagford at this inn. There used to be stables at the back but these have since been replaced by dwellings.

The Ring o' Bells, in The Square, is another fine pub and was one of several featured in Victor Holton's "Hotel Discoveries of 1949." In this guide he wrote: "This small country inn is one of half-a-dozen little red blobs on my map … Your breakfast will come to you in bed, complete with a morning paper, and no extra bobs [he means shillings!] on the bill for this pretty piece of pampering."

The pub has played its part in the history of the area. It was here that the Crowner (or coroner) performed his gruesome task of deciding the cause of death of people in the area. However it was never as simple as that for communications, all those years ago, left a lot to be desired and cross-country journeys in Devon were wearisome, time-consuming affairs and the Crowner for Chagford lived some twenty-five miles away in Black Torrington. In cases where people died suddenly or where there was suspicious circumstances, a parish constable was obliged to take the details to the Crowner. That journey, in all seasons and in all weathers was often a difficult one in the early 1800s. For years it fell on the tender shoulders of George Clampitt, a boot and shoe maker, who needed to have faith in his own footwear as he was often called upon to road test them!

As soon as he heard of a death of the type specified he, the Crowner's messenger, would don his uniform and set off to Okehampton some eleven miles distant. Being a man of regular habit he would make for the aptly named 'George Inn' (there was no Clampitt Arms in Okehampton!), and having had his fill he would struggle on the fourteen miles to Black Torrington to deliver his message to the Crowner. He, in turn, would give instructions to George Clampitt to arrange with the landlord of the Ring O' Bells to book a date and an upper room there for the crowning. For this a twelve man jury was summoned to adjudge the circumstances of the deceased's demise. In the case of suicides it was decreed that they should not be buried in consecrated ground. If the verdict was 'felo de se', that is self-murder, the funeral took on a macabre appearance. The body was taken in the dark and by lanternlight, to a crossroads, that being the sign of the cross. Two grave diggers would have prepared a grave and two sets of bearers would take the corpse to its last resting place where no service would be performed. The Crowner's messenger had to see through the case to the conclusion, having to witness the burial and the filling in of the grave even through to seeing it returfed.

The two most famous recorded instances of this procedure on Dartmoor concern poor Kitty Jay, buried near Hound Tor and unfortunate George Stephens who lies on the moor above Peter Tavy, a village on the western side of the moor. You can read more of these sad suicides in some of our other Dartmoor titles! Originally there was a Ring of Bells in Mill Street but this inn burnt down in 1860.

The Buller's Arms when it was The Baker's Arms

There are plenty of places for alcoholic refreshment in Chagford, possibly the reason why my beer-drinking baptism was in this moorland town at a tender age… However all that walking on Dartmoor is very thirst-provoking and Chagford's pubs have a certain indefinable quality that makes the consumption of ale an even more pleasurable experience. Long ago there were even more pubs but market forces, changing social habits and even ferocious fires have depleted their numbers. The Three Canons fell into the last category, being burnt to a shell in 1835. The story goes that a

Chagford miller chanced upon a crock of money and used some of it to buy the ruined site of this pub. In its place he built Canon House.

In those days there was a Royal Oak Inn at The Square and outside a stream ran across this open space. Two stones were located, one near the Royal Oak and the other outside the building that is now Lloyds Bank, to enable packhorses and cattle to cross without having to get wet. The Royal Oak later became a milliner's shop.

On the other side of The Square was the King's Arms that was owned by the Newton Abbot brewers of Pincent. The most unusually named pub in Chagford, and possibly in Devon, was the Swindonia. It was believed to be the only one in the country to possess such a name. All three landlords of the Royal Oak, the King's Arms and the Swindonia had other business interests, all three being butchers by trade and all three had premises at the Shambles or Market House! There was also another inn in New Street that was trading as long ago as 1446 as the White Eagle. Unfortunately this pub became extinct.

The present Buller's Arms was previously called the Baker's Arms but General Buller's achievements in the Boer War prompted a spate of dedications all around the county in the shape of statues, in the naming of streets and public buildings. In this case he was honoured in a pub name. He is buried at Crediton. The change of name coincided with a major refurbishment in 1898 when walls were raised, a new roof added and a bar parlour erected. Two cottages nearby were demolished to make way for the appropriately named Ladysmith House. The latter's entry in the local guide book said: "Put up here for your moorland holidays … very moderate charges, personal supervision and above all, cleanliness."

The Sandy Park Inn is a fifteenth century inn that lies at a crossroads on the road to Castle Drogo, about a mile out of Chagford. At one time it boasted that it possessed the rudest landlord in the country, a Basil Fawlty type. In the past the landlord of this pub was almost invariably a blacksmith with plenty of passing trade to keep him busy. As an older teenager I always had problems playing

darts here as the ceiling was low and the number of times I impaled darts there when going for a double twenty is nobody's business. The pub is well placed for liquid refreshment if on a walk along the River Teign (a perfect excuse).

Nearby is the lovely Mill End Hotel which, as its name suggests, was a mill at one time. One-time mill owner, Frank Rowe, was a member of the Plymouth Brethren and it was a common sight to see baptisms performed in the mill leat there.

Chagford has had many famous visitors. Evelyn Waugh stayed at the Easton Court Hotel and wrote his *Brideshead Revisited* whilst there! Gracie Fields once spent a pleasant weekend break at Chagford, having visited Devon for some performances.

Rolf Harris camped on the lawn of the Beverley Hotel. He came to Devon to woo his loved one, the daughter of the owners, Major and Mrs T. G. Hughes. The rooms all being taken, he tied his tent pegs down, sport, and eventually married Alwyn Hughes.

Even more bizarre was the 'tardy' arrival in town of Dr Who (Tom Baker). This time he exchanged his Tardis for a more conventional mode of travel. The crew had gone to shoot an episode at the quarries near Haytor but a typical Dartmoor deluge caught them by surprise and as the Tardis was not large enough to accommodate them all, they took a coach to Chagford and bought all the rainwear they could get from Webbers in The Square. The late William Hartnell, who was the original Dr Who, has also visited Chagford.

Marconi stayed at the Moor Park Hotel (now converted into cottages) and whilst there gave serious consideration to the idea of putting a radio mast atop Meldon Hill. However he eventually decided to go farther west and a shade closer to America by erecting it on a Cornish hillside instead.

Bamber Gascoigne, the celebrated former question-master of the television quiz "University Challenge" also stayed at the Moor Park. This hotel, at its peak, used to advertise with the slogan "the Best Centre for Touring Dartmoor."

Actress Irene Handl was a frequent visitor up till the time of her death. John Mills, the famous film star stayed at Chagford whilst he made the film "Run Wild, Run Free." On a similar tack Billy Connolly and Michael Caine took time off from the filming of "Water", a film that starred Leonard Rossiter, shortly before his death, and which was filmed in and around Hartland in North Devon. They visited Chagford for the day and signed autographs for locals who recognised them. Not a lot of people know that! More details of these and many other films and television programmes made in this county can be discovered in another of my books, *Made in Devon*.

One of the oldest visitors must have been the playwright, Ben Travers, who was nearly a hundred years old at the time! The authoress, Mary Wesley (Mrs Seipman) was not so much a visitor but a resident as she lived near Chagford at Teigncombe, but she eventually forsook the moorland life to go and live in 'the Good Town of Totnes.'

Then there were those who had little choice but to come to Chagford. Holystreet Manor was occupied during the war by St Monica's of Clacton-on-Sea, as complete a change of environment as could ever be expected for these Essex youngsters. After the

20

war it became a school again under the care and attention of Miss Tompson and Miss Watson, but this time as St Bride's.

There is also a bizarre story about two Edwardian ladies who came down to London for a short stay at a Chagford hotel. Their purpose was to see what they thought of the place and if they liked the area to find somewhere to stay for a

Some of the buildings at Holystreet Manor

holiday. Well, how can anyone not fall in love with a place like this? After some searching they found their dream cottage, and they arranged with the owner (a slightly old fashioned but genteel lady), a mutually acceptable date for them to rent the cottage for a short holiday. But when they returned to check some small detail … the cottage did not exist!

Chagford's pride and joy is its Market House, which stands as a most distinct landmark in The Square and is featured on most postcards of the town and almost every edition of every guide book! However it is not an easy building to photograph as it is invariably surrounded by parked cars, probably the reason why it is often drawn instead, the artist possessing the power to remove unsightly signs, street furniture, traffic and that odd person who likes to walk in front of the camera at that crucial moment when the shutter is clicked!

The original building on this spot suffered an ignominious ending on Friday, 6 March 1617 and its demise is a poignant reminder, to all upstanding Chagfordians and visitors alike, that fate rarely needs little tempting.

The Stannary Court was in session and before it was a dubious character giving evidence of a less than convincing nature, a story so beyond belief that he was reminded, in no uncertain terms, that to lie on oath was a serious matter. To this he replied that, "If I am lying may God bring the roof down on my head in judgment!" Needless to say he must have been telling a whopper for immediately the whole place collapsed, the walls falling in whilst the roof crashed down killing the man and nine more who were present. Amazingly, whilst some tough strong men were crushed to death a small baby survived the ordeal and was pulled safely from the wreckage. Although a structural weakness was no doubt made to give by the number of people in the building, the timing and the drama

of the situation makes one think! Chagford, just for the record, has endured the occasional earthquake with at least three strong shakes in the 1860s.

The present Market House had its foundation stone laid in 1862, an occasion of celebrations and speeches. It was reported in various papers and it was expected that this sparkling new edifice would "promote an intellectual taste among the young people of Chagford, and teach them that there was a better and pleasanter way of passing the long winter evenings than in wasting their precious time in the public houses." The notion being that a reading room here would provide a more stimulating experience, perhaps a forerunner to evening classes! Designed by Mr Herbert Williams, of London, this building stores some inaccessible treasures. History relates that "Mr Ormerod then placed on a hollow of the lower stone a glass tube containing photographic views of the old Market House and a list of parish officers and building committee. This being covered with a metal plate, Mrs Hames was presented with a trowel, with which she spread the mortar; the stone then slowly descended as the band played the National Anthem."

At the end of the proceedings: "Three cheers were then cordially given for Mrs Hames and the ladies, and these were followed by cheers for the rector (Mr Hames), the Lord of the Manor the churchwardens and Mr Ormerod. The band then struck up a lively march, and the meeting, the largest that had taken place at Chagford in many years, then dispersed."

The Market House was given a major overhaul in 1984, in particular the roof needed much attention. When it was taken off, hundreds of pigeon eggs were discovered! Despite this a new lid was added and the nickname of 'the Pepperpot' was bestowed upon it, pretty hot stuff!

It's amazing how some buildings change functions. There can't be too many thatched banks in this country. Chagford's Lloyds Bank is therefore a rare building that has seen a number of uses down the years. The building's deeds go back to the middle of June 1735 but it was obviously one of little assets for when it changed hands in 1802 it was described as being 'a decayed house'. For several years it was a blacksmiths' shop but in 1842 it was converted into two cottages. Lloyds acquired the property in 1918 so we guess that the mortgage is well paid up by now!

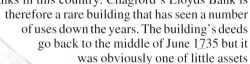

The National Westminster Bank building was, in 1860, the premises of W. A. Gilbey's wine and spirits shop. A case of one set of liquid assets eventually giving away to another!

Another to witness a change of scene and scope is the Rex Gallery in Store Street, which today sells pictures but in the past it showed moving ones! This was the Rex Cinema, a place where many a Chagford old timer had a good time, or so they tell me, until the time it closed its doors in the 1950s. In an old Chagford guide book it says "The Rex Cinema – Open Wed, Thurs, Fri, Sat. Times of showing, see handbills and posters in The Square." Many locals remember the cavernous dark and the flickering pictures of this entertainment emporium. The entertainment was made even more complete for courting couples as there were a number of double seats so that they could be that bit closer together in the dark – oh those Chagford nights!

However you would have to be classified as a real ancient Chagfordian to recall the Magic Lantern Shows that were presented by Mr John Webber at the Methodist Chapel in the days when even this was an amazing spectacle.

Endecott House, in the High Street, between the Globe and the Three Crowns, is another of Chagford's ancient granite buildings with a history. It has had other names and a multitude of uses over the years. Some will refer to it as the Legion Hall whilst others will recall it as St Catherine's Hall. It has also been the Old School but the name Endecott House was introduced to reflect that it was neither the sole domain of the church nor Royal British Legion. The choice of name is adopted from a Chagford man who went on to become the first Governor of Massachusetts Bay in 1644.

St Michael's Parish Church makes an attractive landmark and can be seen from quite a distance. It was

dedicated by Bishop Bronscombe on 30 July 1261. The bishop has a hill near Meldon Reservoir, called Branscombe's Loaf, named after him. The bulk of the church is more recent, dating back to the fifteenth century. Within it are memorials to several leading families. It is a place for quiet prayer and meditation. One attractive feature, that is often missed, lies in a niche just below the clock face on the tower. It's a statue of St Michael and is the work of the late John Skeaping who, at one time, was a resident of Chagford.

In the graveyard is a fine war memorial. It too has a history having started life as the market cross that stood in The Square. Eventually it found its way (with a little bit of human assistance!) to Holystreet where it remained until a monument was required to honour the dead of the Great War.

Despite its lack of size Chagford has had, and continues to have, many places of worship. The Ebenezer Gospel Hall in Southcombe Street was originally opened,

24

in 1827, as a Baptist chapel. About 1900 it was run by the old Bible Christians but had a change of direction when it changed hands and became an Open Brethren place of worship. In the late 1970s it was handed over by the Lake family to be run by a small number of trustees.

There are also other long-established denominations represented in Chagford.

Between the Ebenezer Gospel Hall and The Square there is a forking of the ways where 'the fountain' is sited. The water trough was presented to the town in 1889 and was no doubt a welcome sight for some arriving in town in those days. Behind it is a tiny building, regarded as the smallest shop in Chagford. This was once the workshop of the town's last cobbler, A. W. Lyddon, whose small firm existed for several generations.

Despite its intrinsic beauties, getting to Chagford has never been easy particularly on public forms of transport. Half my youth seems to have been spent on Devon General buses wending their way from Exeter to the moorland town. From Chagford's Square to Exeter's bus station is a tad under fifteen miles as the crow flies. The bus route that my Dartmoor walking friends and I were taken on, in the mid 1960s, between these two places was double that and it took just a pinch under two hours to complete a journey that deviated to take in places like Bridfordmills and Dunsford. In fact almost any place that was unlikely to add to the number of passengers being conveyed! The worst aspect of the return journey was that it was often under-taken after the consumption of several pints of shandy or beer ... getting to Exeter's bus station was a great relief!

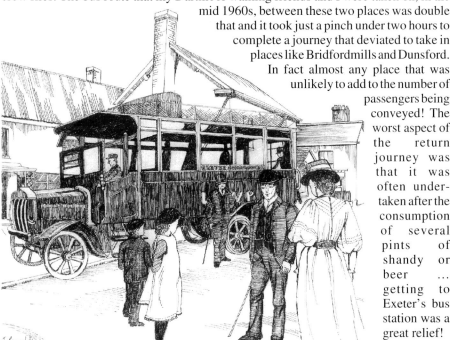

Here I have included the bus timetable for 1925 (just to be topical!) The 40–50 minutes taken between Moreton and Dunsford can't be much slower than the stage coaches of yesteryear! And if your maths are good you will notice that the journey from Exeter out to Chagford, on the uphill journey, was always five minutes more than the other way.

In the early part of the twentieth century a newspaper article proudly boasted that: "Chagford is the only civilised place in close proximity to the Moor." The bus service was, in part, instrumental in the reasoning behind such a bold statement. "The 'bus is a very good vehicle, the horseflesh fair, the driver chatty and agreeable (when in a good temper), the scenery refreshing and the air invigorating." But the length of time it took to get from Exeter to Chagford was still the cause of an amount of bemoaning and groaning. The last horse-drawn bus ran in April 1906 and, no doubt, some overworked horses were probably relieved to be put out to grass!

It could have all been so different had Chagford been added to the railway network and it came within a whisker of doing so. After all Moreton had become the terminus of the line that ran across the Bovey Basin to Bovey Tracey then up the valley to Lustleigh before following the River Wrey's valley to the line's end hundreds of feet above sea level. Therefore by Chagfordian

logic, if Moreton have got a line then we want one! But in a land of high hills and general remoteness, to find a flat route to the outside world was not going to be easy. However engineers are visionaries and had the schemes that were planned, before there were any rail routes in the county, been developed they would have changed the landscape and the patterns of public transport in the Dartmoor area.

The Devon Record Office has a set of plans that proposes a line, envisaged in 1840, which followed the Teign Gorge westwards from Dunsford and went on across Dartmoor, close to the Warren House and on to Nun's Cross Farm, south of Princetown. From here it was to be almost downhill stuff to Plymouth. However by 1860 first thoughts had become second ones for the scheme looked not to Plymouth but towards Okehampton. The line would go to Gidleigh, Throwleigh, Sticklepath and ever onwards. As we know these grandiose plans failed to reach fruition and, anyhow, had they done so they would have closed down by now just like the majority of branch lines in areas of low population/high car ownership densities.

And we move from things that weren't built to things that were but have faded in the mists of time. High on the hillside above Chagford there used to be a Golf Club, one of nine holes and tremendous views. Unfortunately it seems that players needed one leg longer than the other to play it as it contoured the slopes of Meldon Hill, one that is precipitously steep in places. The golf course was opened on 8 June 1908 and the Ward Lock Guide for the 1920s reveals that play on a Sunday was only after 1.00 p.m. The annual subscription for Gentlemen was three guineas but for Ladies it was exactly half this amount. Visitors could play for half a crown per day. The Hon. Sec. was Capt. H. Critchley Salmonson. The course extended over some 2,728 yards but with high winds, cussed vegetation and the law of gravity, all ready to play their respective parts, most golfers embarking on a round were in for a much longer trek than that! Alas the Ward Lock Guides of a decade later refer to the only golf course in the district as to that of the Manor House's at North Bovey – somewhere along the line the course proved too much even for those who enjoyed a spot of adventure. When Mr Quick, the club professional, who also performed other practical duties, left in the early 1930s, no replacement could be found and the club closed.

Those with a trained eye can work out the former layout of the course and identify some of the greens. Luke Darlington showed a degree of resolution when he embarked, in recent years, to play a round on this long defunct course. Recording a highly respectable card of 67 for the nine holes, he did, in the process, manage to lose eight balls. That's about one for each letterbox secreted on this immense hill.

But this golf course was history several years before the storm clouds of war gathered over Europe for the second time this century. The Home Guard had various lookouts on high points in the district. One was atop Meldon Hill, the best vantage point for miles around. A hut was placed there for watches in inclement weather. However it was perched on the edge of the steepest part of this 'gert' hill and it's fortunate that in the storm that sent it crashing down the hillside there was nobody in residence. This was probably because the conditions were so bad that no enemy planes could have been spotted anyway! There was another bizarre incident when two Royal Engineers tried to demonstrate the use and effectiveness of a Bangalore Torpedo. (This, for those unfamiliar with such matters, was a drainpipe filled with explosives and used as a gun.) However, instead of discharging this weapon into the many acres of Meldon moorland, where little damage would have been done, apart from the risk of killing an unfortunate grazing animal, the fire was misdirected towards Meldon Road. Here many houses had their windows blown in by the blast and the military were obliged to cough up the funds and make the necessary repairs. At the bottom of Meldon Hill there was a tramway constructed so that anti-

New Street

tank guns could practice their shooting skills at a moving target. This would account for the many suspicious metal obstacles dug up here in the intervening years.

Perhaps the most unusual incident of the war involved a retired major who was doing his bit for the defence of the realm. He was on duty at Kestor, hardly a strategic target for the German forces, when out of the dark came footsteps getting ever near. Despite the warnings to stop approaching, the standard "Halt! Who goes there?" line was not heeded. The approaching 'enemy' let out a cough. "Halt or I fire" fell on deaf ears so the major blasted away into the night. The startled, 'invading,' but deeply shocked sheep, shot straight back onto the moor.

Kestor looks down on Chagford from on high and is one of the most individual rockpiles on the moor, an obvious landmark for all who live and work in this quarter of the National Park. Strangely it has an unusual but tenuous connection with the West Indian island of Antigua. The Goole Shipbuilding and Repairing Company, of Yorkshire, were commissioned to build a large motor vessel in 1936. She was 135 foot long, nearly twenty-five foot wide and over seven and a half foot deep. Her owner had a connection with this area so called her MV *Kestor*. She too played her part in the war but survived and was last heard of in the Caribbean where, after a change of name, rejoices in the title *Miss Antigua*, a real beauty! Harrison's, who had originally commissioned her, presented a model to the people of Chagford. Less fortunate was her sister ship – MV *Chagford*! She was built a year later than MV *Kestor* but in March 1938 collided with another vessel off Newhaven and sank, her cargo of stones ensuring that she went straight to the bottom of the English Channel, to lie in one of the busiest shipping channels in the world.

Today it is not regarded as politically correct to have fur farms, but there used to be one between Teigncombe and Kes Tor, a few miles from Chagford. The Wild Pine Fur Ranch, as it was called, was set up in 1919 by an ex-army officer. It was the first silver-fox fur farm in the country, there being only one other in Britain. Some five years after it had begun trading it was bought by a man called Johnstone who promptly changed its name from a western-sounding establishment to a more mundane "Dartmoor Fur Farms." However, the demand for fox furs declined and the enterprise ceased in 1942 when young fashionable ladies had more to think about than draping a dead fox around their necks. For a while skunks were kept and bred there but the less said about that the better.

But getting back to Meldon Hill, which apparently means Middle Hill, it has always played a part in local life, its very dominating presence always hard to ignore. No doubt it has afforded Chagford a certain amount of shelter from strong, gale force winds blowing from a southerly direction. But for most it has provided a challenge, a stiff climb to get the adrenaline pumping, the ideal stroll to blow away those cobwebs. And there are those fitness fanatics who run up this little Devonshire mountain driven by some spiritual force to get to the top as quick as possible before getting back down more quickly. In the Queen's Silver Jubilee year of 1977 the 'Two Hills Race' was inaugurated to enable those with enough puff to race up Meldon and Nattadon in a race of precisely 3.26 miles, involving a total climb of over a thousand feet to reach the top of these peaks. If you can do it in less than thirty-five minutes then you are doing just fine!

These days we are more aware of our heritage and this is evident in many ways from the preservation of old buildings to the revival of old customs. Nostalgia is a modern fad. Many country parishes have gone back to their roots to re-enact the age-old practice of beating the bounds, an activity that probably went out of fashion as maps removed the need to remember where what was and why. It is also likely that the young became a little lazy for such a trek often involved miles of trudging on one of those rare high days or holidays. True the scrumpy eased the pain and, yes, the 'bumping' of singled-out victims caused amusement but all things have a habit of wearing thin and the practice lapsed in many parishes.

However in 1951 it was decided that a renaissance of perambulating around Chagford's far-flung parish bounds was a good idea and the event was resurrected. On that auspicious occasion Mr D. L. Serpell was the oldest participant and it is reported that Mr Underhill was well and truly 'bumped'. This deed was traditionally done to small boys who were bumped on the boundary stones so that they would never forget, once the concussion had subsided or the swelling had gone down, where their parish boundaries ended. 'Angelic' choirboys were often a prime choice for this ritual. The Chagford assembly of 1951 set out from Jurston Green and places en route included Hurston Ridge Farm, Fernworthy Dam and Chagford Bridge.

In the past visiting soccer and cricket teams to Chagford must have thought the playing surface was simply a continuation of Dartmoor as the Padley Common's War Memorial Fields venue, at the bottom of Meldon Hill, left a lot to be desired. Although those who played on it every week, or so, were familiar with its idiosyncrasies and felt local knowledge was worth a few goals start or a few wickets or runs on the score board, there were the purists who wanted to see skill rather than enterprise and endeavour. George Best or Ryan Giggs could hardly have shown the full range of their repertoire on the old Padley Common pitch and it's doubtful if any test batsmen could have guaranteed a big score on the former batting strip. But all that has changed now after many years of planning and subsequent hard work. Chagford's playing surface is as flat as East Anglia and plays better than many professional pitches. Indeed when Torquay United played a special match there, there was an element of envy as it was discovered by the league team that Chagford's pitch was flatter and truer than theirs at Plainmoor. To achieve this 3,300 cubic metres of peat bog had to be sorted out.

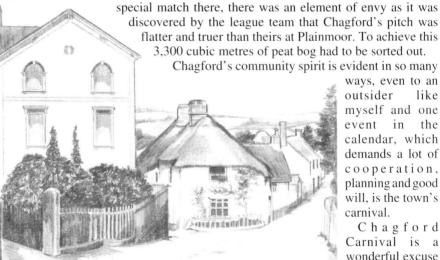

Chagford's community spirit is evident in so many ways, even to an outsider like myself and one event in the calendar, which demands a lot of cooperation, planning and good will, is the town's carnival.

Chagford Carnival is a wonderful excuse for a lot of fun and every year those with a creative flair come up with new ideas. One of the wackiest was many years ago, way back in 1982. As it was National Maritime Year it was felt that it would be appropriate to add a regatta to the proceedings. Although it rains a lot over the hills of Dartmoor, it was obvious that there would never be enough water in the River Teign so Chagford Regatta took place on dry land, much like the one they have at Alice

Springs in the parched interior of Australia. The 'Boat Race' took place on 29 August of that year with legs, rather than oars, propelling the winning crews to victory.

The people of Chagford have long known how to have a good time. The field that became the market was known locally as 'Doggyclose' and was the venue for travelling shows, fairs, fêtes and firework displays. There were even winter carnivals when a special attraction was the release of large paper balloons, some six feet in diameter, inflated by hot air from a paraffin burner. Successful ones soared impressively into the sky but those that caught fire only raised a few excitable screams.

The Chagford Show has been an important event since 1898 and one that draws crowds of people to the moorland town. It is celebrated for its horses but sheep and cattle add to the aroma and atmosphere of the show. Throughout the years it has attracted some colourful characters and some quite amazing capers have been witnessed in the fields in the vicinity of Rushford Bridge. The Cheese Race also added to the aromatic environment when, in the past, a whole cheese was rolled down the hill with enthusiastic participants in hot pursuit, the first one to catch it being rewarded with the said cheese. However, as can be imagined, the cheese got into such a state that it was hardly much of a prize. Therefore common sense has prevailed and a football, not made of cheese, has replaced it. The winner wins a selection of cheeses.

Our four-legged friends, under 12.2 hands, are invited to run in 'the Dartmoor Derby', a race that entails a frantic three-times-round-the-showground skirmish. Originally this was a race for just genuine Dartmoor Ponies, but this is not the case now.

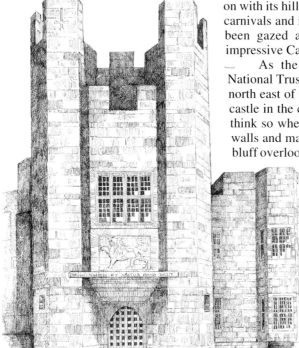

And whilst Chagford has been getting on with its hill runs, its sporting fixtures, its carnivals and its shows, all the while it has been gazed at, from a distance, by the impressive Castle Drogo.

As the Dartmoor crow flies this National Trust property is two miles to the north east of Chagford. This is the newest castle in the country but you would never think so when looking at its stout granite walls and magnificent location on a steep bluff overlooking the Teign's gorge. It has a distinct medieval appearance about it. Such an unusual building is the result of two men of genius and patience, its original owner and its architect.

Julius Drewe was a shrewd businessman who, by the age of thirty-three, had made enough money to retire from the world of commercial enterprise. He made 'pots of money' from being the first importer of tea from India. He made another fortune from his involvement in 'the Home and Colonial Stores'. But sometimes money isn't the be all and end all and Julius set his sights on other achievements, not least creating a home in the area where his ancestors lived.

Having found and purchased the land, Julius made stringent enquiries as to whom the best man would be as architect to turn his dreams and aspirations into reality. There could only have been one choice, a man with an impeccable pedigree, Edwin Lutyens.

Julius wasn't content to have a typically large and comfortable country home built in conventional fashion. For him it was to be a castle and not a lot of those were being built in the first half of the twentieth century.

Having discovered that his ancestors, derived from those who followed and supported William the Conqueror, had given their 'Drogo' or 'Dru' to the village of Drewsteignton, he made a firm commitment to re-establish that link in the most positive of ways. His 'home' was to be a castle that his ancient descendants may have dreamt of but never saw.

By the time this project had got off the ground Julius Drewe, at the age of fifty-four, was old enough to know his own mind and knew exactly what he wanted. However, although a wealthy man, he had a budget and circumstances ultimately decided that the finished article was only a fraction the size of the building that was first envisaged.

Edwin Lutyens was also a man who knew his own mind so this building, which was for twenty years in the making, yielded a lot of interesting discussions and correspondence as it rose from the rough and rugged hillside.

In 1915 Julius asked for a drive that was lined with heather, bracken, broom, holly, brambles, foxgloves and the alike. Lutyens turned to Miss Gertrude Jekyll who, despite her failing eyesight and advanced years, produced a planting scheme. The end result is one of the most attractive approaches gradually rising from the road with views to the left of Drewsteignton to eventually peer over and into the Teign's steep gorge whilst sweeping around to the castle.

Lutyens was in great demand as an architect and in the time that Castle Drogo was being pieced together like some giant granite jigsaw, he was involved in many other projects. These ranged in scale from modest monuments to works of great prestige like the Viceroy's Palace in India.

But even great men sometimes forget quite fundamental things. Lutyens embarked on the building of Castle Drogo having forgotten to obtain the necessary local planning permission! This was soon remedied and the work proceeded. A staggering 28,000 trees were planted, enormous quantities of rock were removed from the site and then equally enormous loads of granite were brought in from various quarries on the moor – Blackingstone near Moretonhampstead, Merrivale and Pew Tor near Tavistock.

Whilst Castle Drogo was being built Julius rented (and later bought) a house called Kilmorie. This was another magnificent house, located on the cliffs above Meadfoot Bay at Torquay. Its own claim to fame was that it was in such an exposed situation facing the prevailing south westerlies it became the only property in Devon to have triple glazing!

As Castle Drogo progressed it was realised that it had its own problems with the weather. It had been built without cavity walls, with no bricks and in a traditional style. However Dartmoor's excessive rainfall soon began to penetrate the joints and, despite waterproofing work, this proved to be a problem for many decades.

The castle took twenty years to build. The First World War (1914-18) stripped the building of its workforce but struck an even crueler blow to its owner. Julius' oldest son, Adrian, was killed in Flanders, in action, in 1917, aged just twenty-six. Visitors to the castle will be able to see a room set aside to his memory.

This tragic loss had a devastating effect on his parents. Julius never really came to terms with his loss and it's believed that this took its toll on his own health with a number of strokes rendering him something of an invalid. He had just a few years to enjoy his castle and died at Torquay in 1931. He lies buried in the churchyard at Drewsteignton, his grave marked by a memorial designed by Lutyens.

Castle Drogo stayed in the family's hands until 1974 when Anthony Drewe and his son gave the house and 600 acres to the National Trust.

A visit is always a pleasure with the added joy of exploring the countryside around it. There are numerous paths and walks to explore with the ramble down to Fingle Bridge a favourite with many. Castle Drogo and Chagford are both set in beautiful countryside and there are many walks along lanes and tracks, over commons and moorlands that both visitors and locals alike can enjoy. The visitor to Chagford hasn't got to travel far for there is a lot of beauty to be discovered in the district. Two miles north the unusual Spinsters' Rock, built they say before breakfast by some Gargantuan women, is an ancient monument with public access, well worth a visit.

Fernworthy Reservoir lies on that proverbial 'road to nowhere' but opens up all sorts of recreational possibilities. There are some lovely hamlets hidden from the mainstream and maelstrom of life in narrow lanes designed, quite possibly, by a drunkard. There is Throwleigh, almost up to the open moor, with its wonderful cottages and impressive church but, unlike Widecombe, which is of a comparable size, there is no folk song or legend and consequently very few visitors.

In this brief look at Chagford and environs we have discovered some of its ghost stories, heard just a little of its history, met some of the characters and visited some of its buildings. In a small book you can never portray everything and everyone. All you can do is try to capture the mood and the flavour of the place. It is true that Chagford is a small place, just a tiny name on most maps, but, as these stories and anecdotes bear out, there are few places, anywhere in Devon, that can match its obvious charm and appeal.